The King and His Three Daughters

How Karma Dictates Everyone's Life

Adapted from a story told by Sant Ram Singh Ji
August 6, 2015

Illustrated by Carlos Brito

"We are the makers of our own fate."
Sawan Singh, Spiritual Gems

GO JOLLY
BOOKS

The King and His Three Daughters:
How Karma Dictates Everyone's Life

The King and His Three Daughters was originally told by
Sant Ram Singh Ji on August 6, 2015 at
Channasandra Ashram in India.

Special thanks to those who commented on, transcribed, critiqued and/or reviewed the story:
Geoff Halstead, Kathryn Boulet, Bob Pearsall,
Richard and Sharon Malarich.
Their suggestions have made the story
more accessible for children.

Translated by Ashok Shinkar
Transcribed by Ali Czernin, Geoff Halstead, & Harvey

Edited by Carol Thompson

Carlos Brito presents brilliant illustrations and an exceptional talent for color combinations that bring joy to our hearts and uplift our
spirits.
Thank you, brother.

ISBN-13: 978-1-942937-06-7

Published by
Go Jolly Books
74 Gem Ln., Sandpoint, ID 83864
FIRST EDITION, GO JOLLY BOOKS, First Printing 2016
10 9 8 7 6 5 4 3 2 1 Printed in the U.S.A.

The King and His Three Daughters

How Karma Dictates Everyone's Life

INTRODUCTION

In January 2014, at Channasandra Ashram in India, I asked Sant Ram Singh Ji (Baba Ji) if I could take stories He told in Satsang and publish them as books.

Although I don't recall His exact words, He said yes. Then He told me to make sure the books were for children. To me that meant I could substitute "Hindi words translated into English words" with "child-friendly English words" to make the story easier for children to understand. With His
Limitless Grace, reviewers have told us we have succeeded.

In March 2016, while visiting with my niece, I told her the story of The King And His Three Daughters. It deeply affected her as she began to see the possibility of viewing life from a new angle of vision, one that includes the major role karma plays.

She seemed to grasp at a deep level what karma and fate karma meant for her and how she might release the stress, anxiety, and disappointment that certain relationships and life cause her.

Her response was the impetus to turn Sant Ram Singh Ji's story into an illustrated picture book, which you are now holding in your hands or listening to.

I hope you enjoy The King And His Three Daughters: How Karma Dictates Everyone's Life. It's been a joyous journey watching Carlos add his colorful, unique illustrations to Baba Ji's words.

Radhaswami,
Harvey

The King and His Three Daughters

How Karma Dictates Everyone's Life

This book is dedicated to Sant Ram Singh Ji,
Whose Limitless Grace and Unconditional Love
show glimpses of what awaits us
upon our return to our Eternal Home.
He is a True Friend and Living Master.

Once upon a time in the state of Punjab in the country of India, there lived a king who had three daughters.

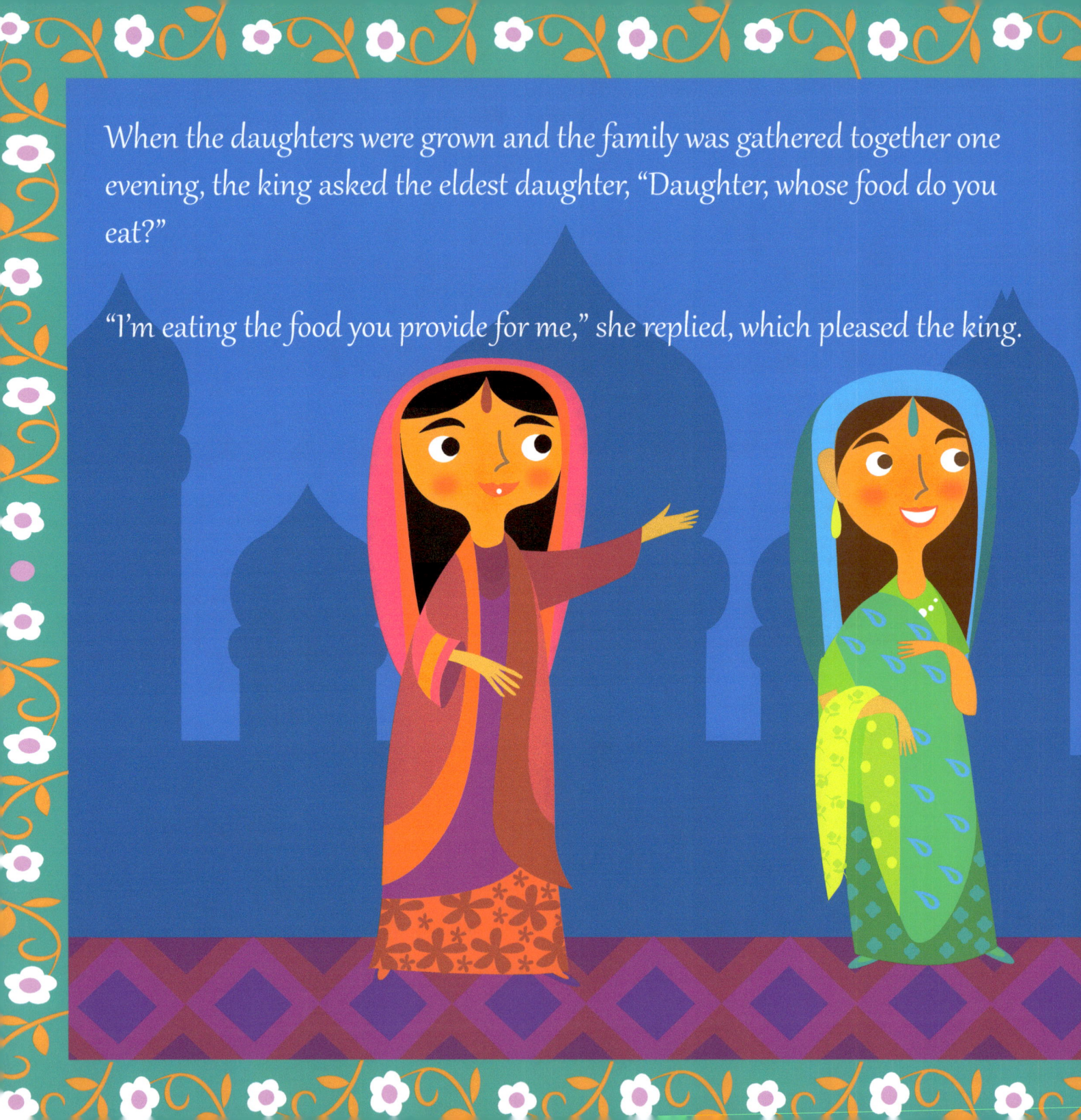

When the daughters were grown and the family was gathered together one evening, the king asked the eldest daughter, "Daughter, whose food do you eat?"

"I'm eating the food you provide for me," she replied, which pleased the king.

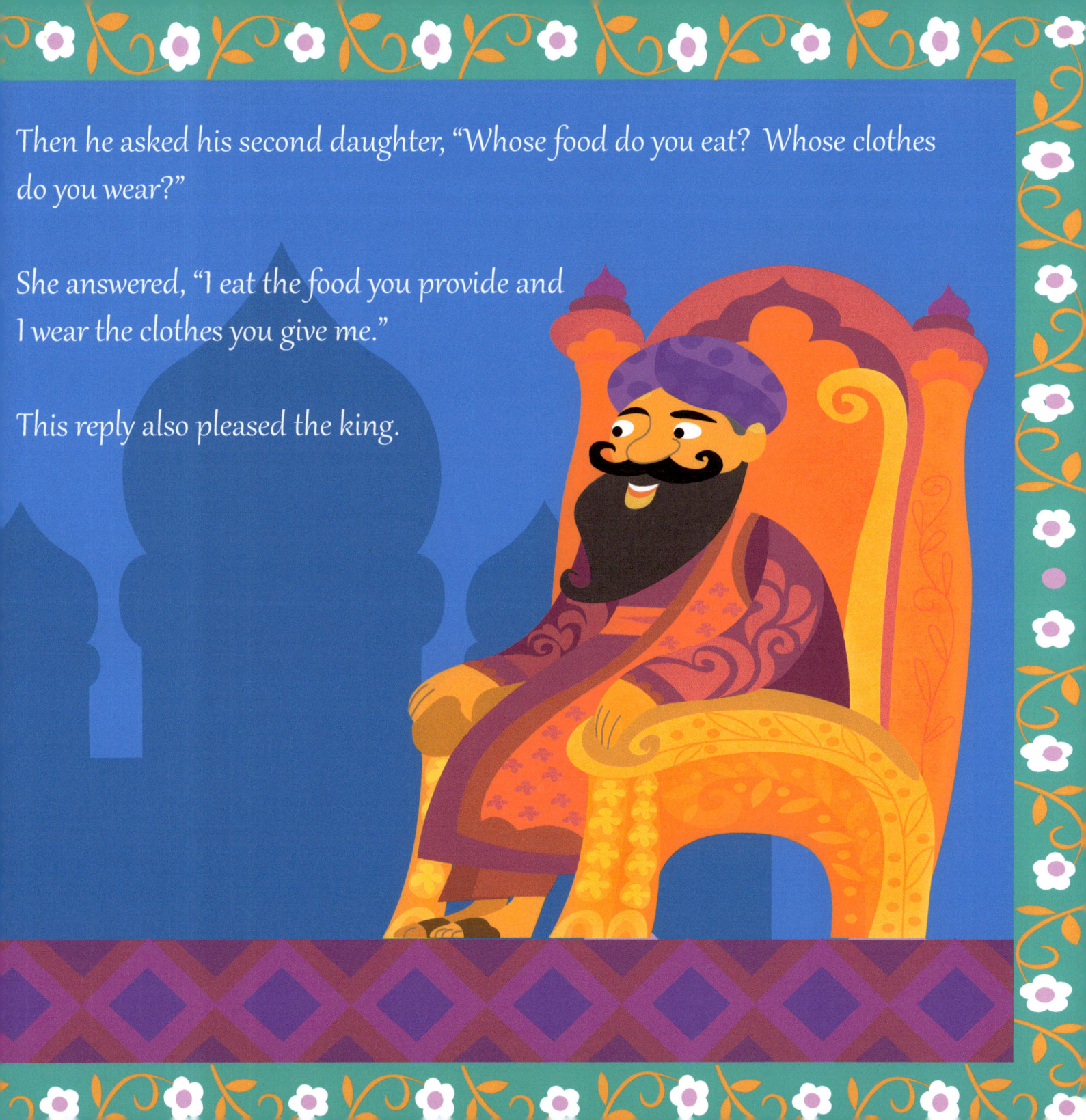

Then he asked his second daughter, "Whose food do you eat? Whose clothes do you wear?"

She answered, "I eat the food you provide and I wear the clothes you give me."

This reply also pleased the king.

Next he asked his youngest daughter, "Whose food do you eat?"

"I'm eating my own food. Whatever food is in my fate for me to eat, I eat that," she answered.

The king thought to himself, "She is too proud and selfish. She doesn't respect that I am her father and the king and I provide all this food for her."

Her words upset the king very much.

As time passed, the king arranged for his two eldest daughters to be married to boys from wealthy families.

When it was time for the youngest daughter to marry, he instructed his pundit saying, "Look, she is from a princely family so find a rich boy for her, but he must be diseased. He should have either leprosy or some sort of serious illness."

The pundit started looking for a rich boy who met the requirements. After searching for a year, the pundit found a prince who had leprosy.

The king was happy. Nobody noticed that the boy's feet and hands were deformed and covered with leprosy as he was wearing shoes and gloves so neither his fingers nor toes could be seen.

So, with a lot of celebration, the marriage ceremony occurred.

When the girl went to her new husband's home, she realized that he had leprosy, but she did not complain to her father. She thanked God Almighty, understanding that it was in her fate that such a boy was to marry her, and she happily accepted the marriage.

After a few months, she decided they should go on a pilgrimage to search for a cure for her husband's suffering. She built a small cart with wheels and a basket where her husband could sit while she pulled it because he could not walk very far.

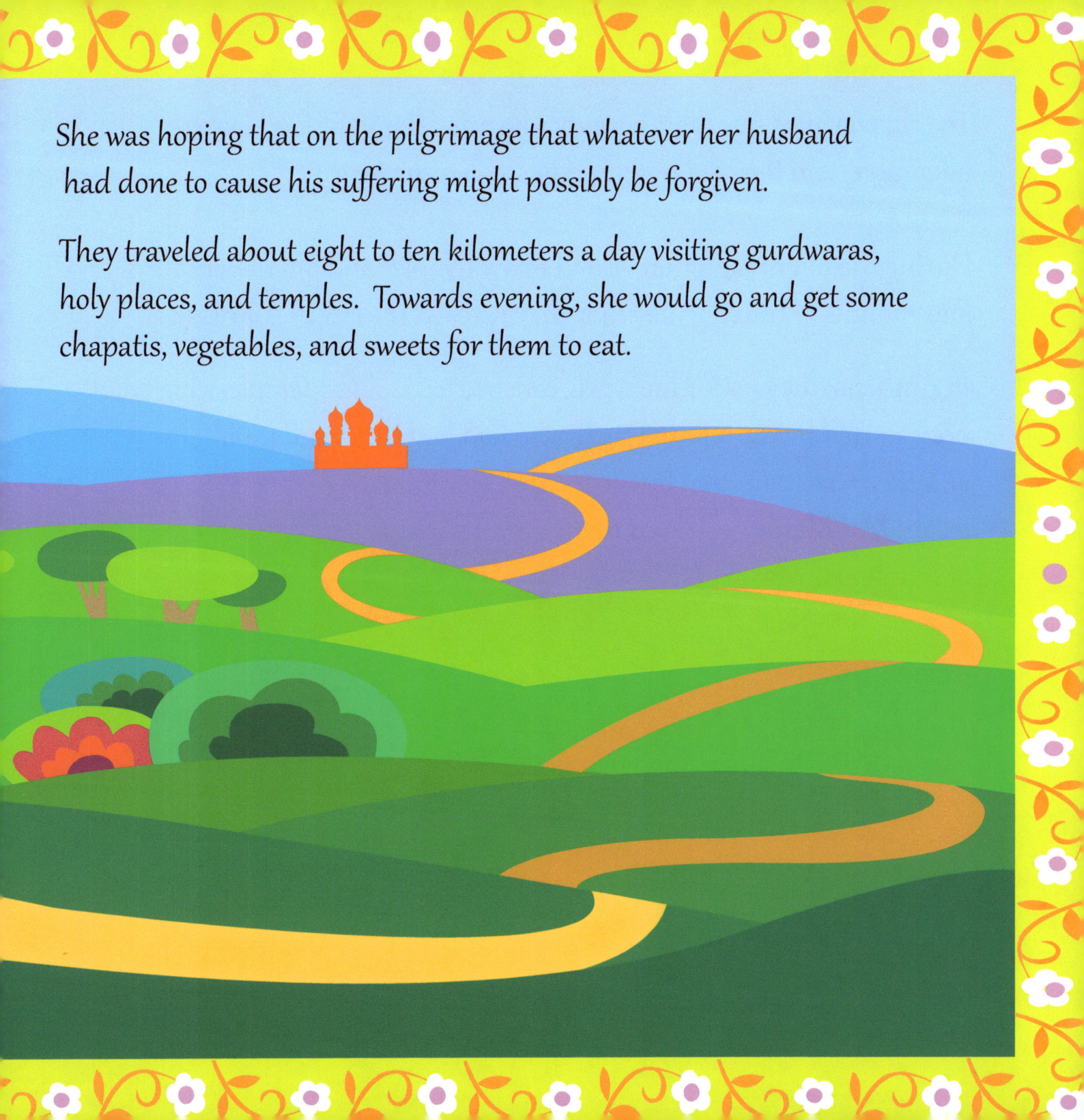

She was hoping that on the pilgrimage that whatever her husband had done to cause his suffering might possibly be forgiven.

They traveled about eight to ten kilometers a day visiting gurdwaras, holy places, and temples. Towards evening, she would go and get some chapatis, vegetables, and sweets for them to eat.

The shop owners saw that this lady who was asking for food looked honorable, and they did not mind giving her the food.

During the pilgrimage, they visited many temples and after about three to four months of traveling like this, they reached the city of Amritsar.

In Amritsar, they visited the newly constructed Golden Temple, which had been started by Guru Ram Das Ji, who had laid the foundation and then was completed by Guru Arjan Dev Ji, a Sant Mat Master, who lived there at that time.

At the Golden Temple, she decided to leave her husband and the cart in the shade of a small tree while she went to ask for food.

While sitting in the cart, her husband saw something very unusual. He saw black crows dip into a pond and then reappear as white crows.

When he saw this happening, he thought, "There must be some power in this water because I am seeing these black crows becoming white."

And so he crawled painfully and slowly to the pond and bathed in the water. As soon as he did this, his karmas were forgiven, and his body turned back into the way it was before he was sick with leprosy.

After he had bathed, he got out of the water and went back to the cart and because he was all wet and his leprosy was gone, he looked like a different person.

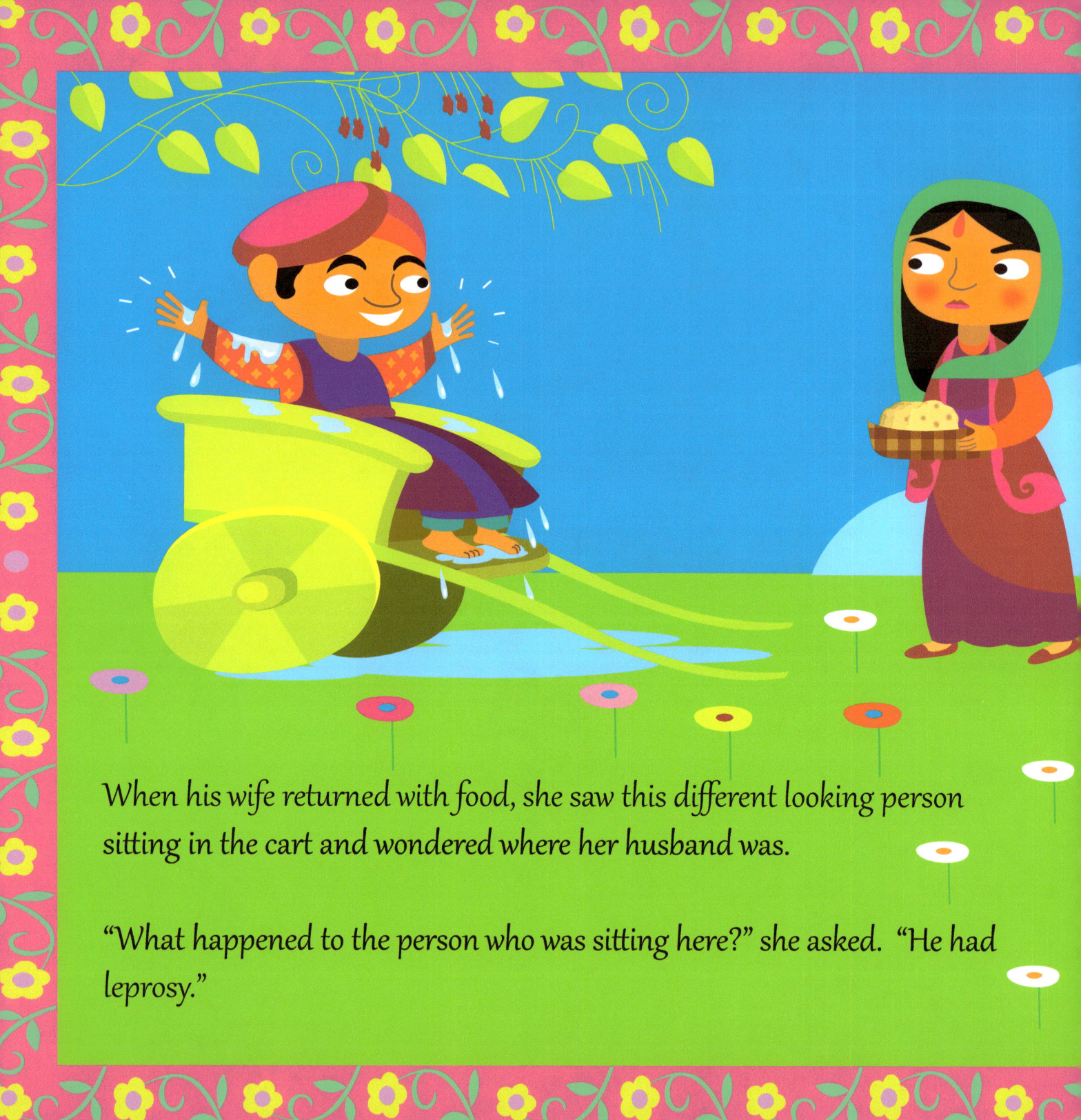

When his wife returned with food, she saw this different looking person sitting in the cart and wondered where her husband was.

"What happened to the person who was sitting here?" she asked. "He had leprosy."

"Look, it is me!" he exclaimed.

"No, no, no, he had leprosy. You look very strong and fit. What have you done with him?"

He explained the whole thing to her; how he saw black crows becoming white, and how he had crawled to the water and taken a bath. He told her there was something special about this pond because his karmas were forgiven and he was changed.

She refused to believe him completely. They argued so loudly that they were both taken to Guru Arjan Dev Ji, who explained to her, "What he is saying is right."

So, their pilgrimage was successful and they returned to his home. His parents were very happy to see what had happened to him and they made him the new king.

He ruled the kingdom fairly with her as his queen.

After some time she felt that she should visit with her father because she had not seen him for a long time. So she sent a brahmin with a horse cart to fetch him.

Her father, the king of Punjab, was feeling bad for what he had done to his daughter. "Just because she said once that she was eating food that is fated for her, I judged her wrongly. I made a big mistake when I arranged for her to marry a man with leprosy."

When that brahmin came with the invitation, her father was quite pleased to go with him to visit his daughter.

When he arrived at the palace, he was treated very well and with a lot of respect. He was even made to sit on a throne.

Soon, both the husband and wife went to her father who was weeping all this time. He said to her, "Look, why are you treating me so well? Why are you honoring me so much when I have actually destroyed your life?"

So then the daughter told her father, "Look, it is not your fault. Don't take it out on yourself. This was all according to my fate karmas. There was something in my fate that caused it all to happen like this.

It is because of devotion to God Almighty that my husband's health is restored and that we have a very blessed and successful life. So please don't blame yourself."

And her father, the king, was very pleased with his third daughter.